# William 'Bill' Bradley

*Addingham's Most Inventive Engineer*

Don Barrett and Ian Crawshaw

First Published 2016
by Addingham Civic Society,
c/o The Old School,
Main Street, Addingham, LS29 0NG
Email: info@addinghamcivicsociety.co.uk

<u>Cover Picture</u>: WB in his workshop in 1970, holding a picture of himself on 'Felix?' at the top of Hepolite Scar (the first sidecar outfit to master it). The picture is now in Bradford Industrial Museum with the bike.

Copyright © 2016 Don Barrett & Ian Crawshaw

All rights reserved.

ISBN-13:978-1523489299
ISBN-10:1523489294

# CONTENTS

|  | Introduction | iii |
|---|---|---|
| Chapter 1 | Early Life | 1 |
| Chapter 2 | The Garage Business | 7 |
| Chapter 3 | Felix? | 13 |
| Chapter 4 | The Family Man | 21 |
| Chapter 5 | Textile Industry | 31 |
| Chapter 6 | The End of The Road | 37 |
| Appendix I | Felix | 43 |
| Appendix II | Felix? | 45 |
| Appendix III | Scott Motorcycles | 51 |
|  | About the authors | 53 |

# William 'Bill' Bradley
(1885 – 1983)
*Seen holding the Yorkshire Gold Medal won for the best invention of 1937*

# INTRODUCTION

This book describes the life of William Bradley from his birth in 1885 to his death at the great age of 98.

The son of an Ilkley plumber, he courageously travelled to Canada at age 19 and after his return, having married an Addingham lass, went on to found his own successful business in Church Street, Addingham; starting as a vehicle repair and servicing garage but later becoming a manufacturer of innovative textile industry equipment.

Bill Bradley was a remarkable engineer. During his long working life, as well as helping numerous motorists with their servicing and repairs, he built complicated and uniquely inventive motorcycles in his successful hillclimbing and cross-country trials riding career. He then successfully took on a challenge to solve some of the problems that beset the local textile industry.

Never daunted by technical problems that lesser people would have deemed impossible to solve, Bill's fertile mind was always coming up with new ideas and solutions and he had the practical skills to turn them into working machines, often at very short notice. An indication that his enquiring mind never left him is the report that at the age of 96 he asked a younger friend to explain how a micro-chip worked!

This book tells of his early life, becoming well known in motorcycling circles for his 'Bradley Special' trials bikes (usually named 'Felix'), his life as a family man and his time as manufacturer of textile equipment at his Beacon Works. The book ends with his final years in retirement and includes appendices giving technical details of his machines.

# CHAPTER 1

# EARLY LIFE

**Plumber's son**

William Bradley was born in Ilkley on the 25th April 1885 to Raper and Rose Bradley.

His father was a plumber with a shop on Skipton Road, Ilkley, and his mother had come up to Ilkley from Peckham, London, to be a lady's sewing maid at 'Summerfield' on South Parade. Some of her brothers had emigrated to Canada, where William was to spend time as a young adult. The family, who lived at Clifton Terrace in Lower Wellington Road (opposite what is now Booths Supermarket), included William's two younger brothers, Harry and Ernest. Raper Bradley was a staunch Methodist and served as a Sunday School Superintendent at the Leeds Road Methodist Church in Ilkley.

William started at the Ilkley National School when he was 4 years old. His mother, sadly, died of rheumatic fever when he was eight but his father remarried. Also outliving his second wife Mary with whom he had a daughter, Emily, he then took a third wife and they had a son, George.

# William 'Bill' Bradley

*Raper and his second wife Mary, with William, Harry & Ernest*

William left school at 14 and started working for his father but he didn't want to stay in his father's business so, at the age of 18, he decided to study engineering, attending an evening course at Bradford Technical College, where he took technical drawing, physics, chemistry and leadwork.

*Raper Bradley outside his plumber's shop in Skipton Rd, Ilkley*

# Addingham's Most Inventive Engineer

However, in 1904, when he was just 19, he adventurously travelled all the way out to Canada to stay with his uncle. He found work as a civil engineer, involved in the construction of a 10" natural-gas pipeline and bridges on the Canadian-Pacific Railroad; roughing it with the other workers, some of them dangerous, knife-wielding fugitives, washing with snow and sleeping in flea-ridden huts.

When he wasn't working, he stayed on his Uncle Will's farm on the Saskatchewan prairie and rode a brown and white pinto pony, bareback. *(In later life he told his grandchildren about his adventures and showed them the scars on his hands from when he had tried in vain to free the pony from a barbed wire fence; bed-time stories certainly weren't boring with WB as a grandfather!)*

William (above) returned to Ilkley in 1907, via New York, and started back working for his father the very next day.

## *First Motorcycle*

Whilst in Canada he had bought himself a Blickens-Döffer typewriter on which to type letters home. He brought the typewriter back with him to England and early in 1908 he swapped it for a box of motor cycle parts. His father had a place in Back Bolton Bridge Road, Ilkley, and there was a draughty 8ft x 8ft corrugated iron hut adjoining these premises where William worked day and night to build a motorcycle from the parts that he had bought, and had it on the road before Easter. This experience was the start of a life-long interest in motorcycles, how they are made, and how to improve them.

The bike that he assembled had a Raleigh frame but was powered by a Dutch made 345cc, 2.75hp, Minerva engine (an engine then used by several motorcycle manufacturers) and he referred to it as a 'Bradley Minerva'. It had three compartments in the tank, for petrol, oil and the fuel/air mixture which was fed to the engine. Petrol then cost just 4.5d (old pennies), or 2p, per gallon! The machine had belt drive and no gears or kick-starter so it was started by pushing vigorously and jumping on when the engine fired.

*Bradley on his self-built 1908 motor cycle.*

On his first outing, which was to York on 'Military Sunday' 1908, he was accompanied by two pals on push bikes who were convinced that he would not make it. He did, but they didn't, as they both had punctures on the way. On his return journey Bill gave one pal a lift back with his bike on his shoulder! He reported that the motorcycle ran for 28 miles before the tank went dry.

## *Marriage*

In 1910 William married Edith Tunnicliffe of Addingham. Her father, John, had a grocers shop on the corner of Church Street and North Street, Addingham, and the newly-weds moved in above the shop with her parents while William continued to work for his father as a plumber.

The Scott motorcycle firm was then established at Saltaire, Bradford and earning a reputation as *the* bike for competition use *(see Appendix III)* so, as Bill enjoyed riding off-road, he desperately wanted a Scott but they were expensive bikes and beyond his means. However, early in 1910, he found a young Scott owner who had bent his mount rather badly in an accident and had had to get a new frame. Bill managed to buy the damaged frame and, proudly, he then owned a piece of a Scott at least, but no engine or radiator!

*North Street in c.1910. Bill's first workshop was at the top of the street*

'*Rather disgracefully, I suppose*', (his words) he fitted a White and Poppe, 3½hp 4-stroke engine *(see box overleaf)*, rather than the correct engine, into the Scott frame, which he had repaired. The W&P engine had a water-cooled cylinder head so he made a radiator, detachable in two halves, out of sheet copper, and also a seat tube petrol tank with two polished copper bands encircling it at the correct angle to make it look like a Scott tank. This kept him mobile, was a step up from his 1908 bike, and enabled him to start exploring the 'rough stuff'. He later, in 1910 to 1911, fitted a sidecar (which cost him £5), but it did not do the Scott frame any good because the roads were poor, the frame was not designed for it, and Bill was inclined to go off-road to find even worse conditions! The bike had no clutch, gears or kick starter but had a good Bosch magneto.

## *War comes*

When the 1914-18 War came Bill made three attempts to join up in the forces but failed because he was deemed unfit due to varicose veins. However, he was involved with the manufacture of aircraft parts at The English Electric Company in Bradford, where he put his inventive mind to good use, and he also joined the Motor Volunteer Force in Ilkley as a dispatch rider, on a 8/10hp, water cooled, Williamson motorcycle.

During and after the War Bill built and/or rode many various outfits, both solo and sidecar, and began to appreciate the short-comings of the current motor cycles in general and side-cars in particular. A challenge for the future!

> **White & Poppe**
> *Alfred White first met Peter Poppe in August 1897 when visiting a small arms factory in Austria. They became friends, and White suggested to Poppe that he moved to Coventry to set up an engine business. The company initially worked on the design of a single cylinder engine but this was interrupted by manufacture of munitions for the Boer war (1899-1902). The first engine produced was for a motorcycle, in 1903 (80mm bore 85mm stroke, air cooled). In 1905 they introduced a 80mm bore 90 mm stroke engine in 2, 3 and 4 cylinder versions (7-14 hp).*

# CHAPTER 2

# THE GARAGE BUSINESS

*Bill Bradley (in the driving seat), and staff, in 1919.
To the left of Bill is his brother-in-law Harold Tunnicliffe who later owned a successful motor car business in Ilkley.*

After the war, in 1919, Bill decided to start his own motorcycle and car repair business. His first workshop was a small building at the top of North Street, Addingham, just up the road from the family home.

In the peaceful post-war years car and motorcycle ownership was becoming more and more common and those in the area able to afford a vehicle took family outings up to Bolton Abbey and beyond, often using North Street on their way through Addingham. As can be imagined, in those early days, there were often breakdowns and Bill became adept at helping maintain and repair his customers' vehicles, often devising and manufacturing improvements to the original design; *'Nothing is impossible'* was his motto. Bill's clever and inventive mind was again showing itself!

This business must have been successful because, after a few years, he was able to buy some land on Church Street, on the corner with North Street, conveniently opposite the shop where he and Edith still lived, now with their three children. The land was bought from Septimus Wray, proprietor of the Pleasure Gardens beside the river in Ilkley, and here Bill built himself a much larger workshop (to be called 'The Beacon Works') for doing vehicle servicing and repairs. He was also a cycle agent & sold petrol *(see photo below)*.

*The Church Street garage in the 1920s. The 'Low' School, in North St, is in the background on the right*

### The Cross Country challenge

As mentioned before, Bill had always been excited by off-road riding and in those days even the roads could be pretty rough!

Having joined the Ilkley & District Motorcycle & Light Car Club in 1919 he started to take part in their events. He particularly enjoyed motorcycle hillclimbs and 'trials' riding; cross country events where the challenge is to ride as far as possible along a marked route over rough, steep, rocky and/or muddy ground, without losing your balance and having to put a foot down or come to a stop. The countryside around Addingham is very suitable for this and events were, and still are, held on Addingham Moorside and other places in the area, as well as elsewhere in the country.

Given his engineering skills and inventive nature, Bill was soon thinking up ways to improve the standard machines of the day. He would modify and make design improvements to his motorbikes, particularly Raleigh & Scott models, on which he became very competitive in club events and this also brought welcome publicity for his business.

In 1924 he had the amazing idea of making the engine drive the **front** wheel as well as the rear so as to give double the traction on muddy and loose surfaces. However, driving the, steering, front wheel from the existing transmission is quite a challenge and to design all the components and manufacture the lot in under two weeks seems a near-miracle, but Bill did it and as far as he was concerned it was just another interesting exercise in precision engineering! This machine did 2,000 miles in a year, at an average speed of 20mph.

This Raleigh motorcycle was modified to compete in the 1924 Southern Scott Trial at Camberley, Surrey, where it acquitted itself very well, winning a Bronze medal. *(This event was an intended rival to the famous north-country classic Scott Trial, see box p.11)*

### 'Felix'

He called his machine 'Felix' and that name was to become synonymous with William Bradley, Engineer, of Addingham.

He achieved the front wheel drive by means of a long chain, driven by a double sprocket, running up the frame to a universal-jointed cross shaft on the handle bars. A sprocket on this shaft drove the front wheel via a second chain. (*The technical details of this, including Bill's own drawings, are included in Appendix I.*) He patented his method of driving the front wheel which he used on Felix and hoped to sell the idea to the army but, in his words, *'the brass hats were not interested in two wheel tanks'*!

> *'Felix the cat' was a famous Disney cartoon character of that era, who always kept on walking despite all attempts to thwart him: 'Blow him up with dynamite and him you cannot kill: With his hands behind him he keeps on walking still' went the lyrics of the popular song of the time. WB's unique Felix motorcycles were to prove equally good at keeping going through the toughest challenges.*

*'Felix'–the front-wheel-driving chain and sprocket can be clearly seen*

He gave a spectacular demonstration, though *'actually dead easy'*, at the Skipton Motorcycle Meet on Good Friday 1924. In a masterly bit of publicity Bill pushed the front wheel up against a house wall and on engaging the clutch Felix proceeded serenely to climb up the wall, not stopping until the rear stand

## Addingham's Most Inventive Engineer

was grounding on the pavement and Bill had stepped off backwards! (right)

Felix was eventually sold to a man at Appletreewick because Bill never stayed with one idea for long and a second Felix was probably more than a glimmer in Bill's eye even as he rode the Raleigh which bore that engaging feline on its front forks.

### *THE SCOTT MOTORCYCLE TRIALS*

*The Scott Trial began in 1914 when Alfred Angas Scott, inventor and founder of the Scott Motorcycle Company, challenged the workers at his factory to ride from the factory in Saltaire through the Yorkshire Dales to Burnsall, a riverside village near Grassington. Of the 14 starters only 9 finished. The event was reintroduced after the First World War, in 1919, and although Alfred Scott died in 1923 the event continued to be run by the Scott workers until 1926.*

*The Bradford and District Motor Club then took over the management of the event and moved the start and finish to Blubberhouses in the Washburn Valley. In 1938 the land was owned by the Leeds Waterworks Authority which decided not to allow motorcycle trials on their property, so the trial was moved again to Swainby, in the north western corner of the North York Moors National Park in Cleveland, and control was taken over by the Middlesbrough and Stockton Motor Clubs.*

# William 'Bill' Bradley

*In 1950 the Auto-Cycle Union, the governing body of motorcycle sport in Great Britain, divided the area into the North Eastern Centre and the Yorkshire Centre and the Scott Trial was moved to Swaledale, where it has remained to this day. The Darlington and District Motor Club took over the organisation until 1990, when the Richmond Motor Club took over.*

*The Scott Trial became the undisputed highlight of the trials season after the 1914-18 war. The Trial took place in the Yorkshire Dales, mainly Wharfedale, Nidderdale and the Washburn Valley, the competitors having to traverse roads, fields, moors and rivers. In the definitive book 'The Greatest of all Trials' by Philip. H. Smith, 1963, he mentions that modifications to bikes by their owners were becoming fairly general and, for example, 'that mechanical genius from Addingham, W. Bradley had equipped his Scott outfit with an extra three speeds and a drive to the sidecar wheel. Not only that, when amphibious operations were imminent, the magneto could be pressurised from the passengers air cushion to keep water out of the sparks!'*

*The 1926 event started and finished at Ilkley, the route took in Addingham Moorside, Draughton, Halton Moor, Barden Bridge, Burnsall, Hebden Ghyll, Grassington Moor and Conistone before a rest interval at Kettlewell. A restart there took them up Park Rash and through Coverdale to Arkleside. Crossing the watershed into Nidderdale, the river was crossed just below Angram, thence down the valley and over to Greenhow, Pockstones Moor, and then into the Washburn Valley at West End where they rode down the riverbed which was known as the West End Staircase (now drowned beneath the reservoir), on via Fewston to Dob Park watersplash, over Denton Moor and back to Ilkley: a total distance of 105 miles. There were dozens of observed and timed sections on the way where competitors lost marks for being late etc. The book tells us that 'Bradley's Scott Special, the last surviving sidecar outfit for many miles, finally called it a day at West End after an incredible performance'. There were only 30 finishers from an entry of 134.*

# CHAPTER 3

# 'FELIX?'

Soon after completing and having success on 'Felix', Bill turned his attention to developing a sidecar outfit, also for trials events and again built to challenge the best in trials competitions. In fact, this outfit achieved even greater fame, and for a much longer period, than the solo Felix. It was 40 years before it was to be retired to the Bradford Industrial Museum, where it can still be seen.

This time he based his machine on a 596cc Scott Squirrel motorcycle and sport sidecar outfit made locally at Saltaire, Bradford. Scott bikes were made for many years and were of a unique design, being two stroke engines with water cooling–very advanced for the time. (*See the Scott Story, Appendix III)*

'Felix?' (the question mark was because you never knew what the bike would do next!) was built specifically as a sidecar outfit, again with trials winning as one object but Bill also wanted an unstoppable towing vehicle with which to rescue the sometimes rather haphazardly constructed cars of the period which their unsuspecting owners had pitted against the Yorkshire wildness!

It was at this time, around 1925, that the A.C.U.(Auto Cycle Union, the sport's governing body) ban on public-road hillclimbs resulted in the opening of two private hills in the district; Hepolite Scar at

Bradford (behind the Hepworth & Grandage works) and Post Hill near Leeds-freak hills with gradients steeper than 1in2. Bill Bradley had an eye on these formidable gradients, '*unclimbable by sidecar'* so they said. Obviously Felix? would have to be an animal of many parts, and so he turned out.

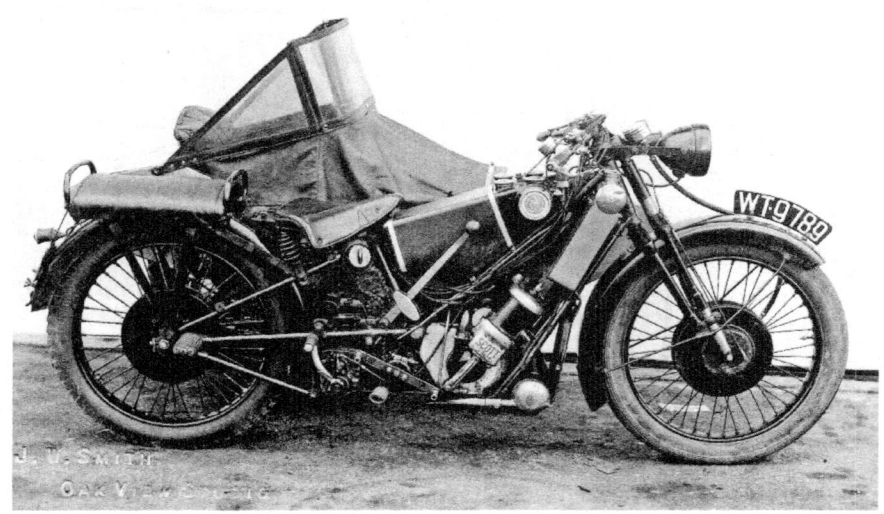

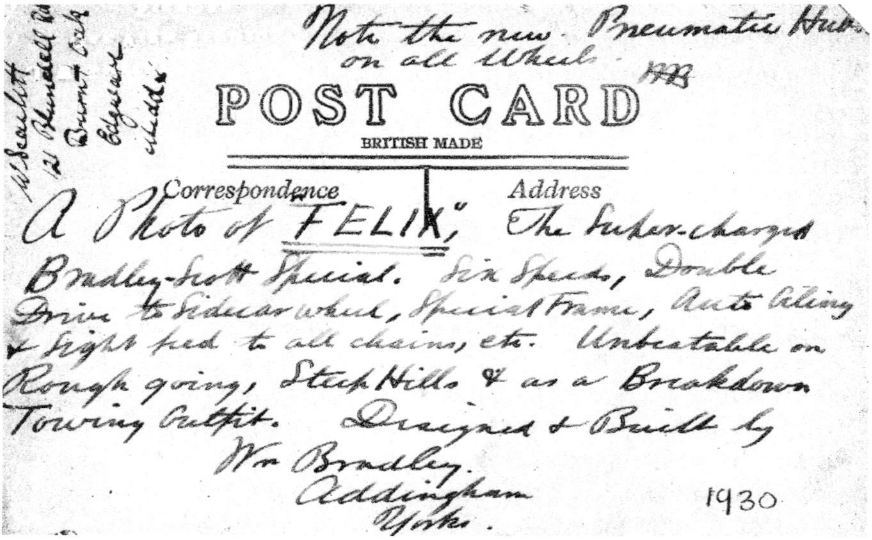

Note the new Pneumatic Hubs on all Wheels. WB

W Scarlett
21 Blundell Rd
Burnt Oak
Edgware
Middx.

POST CARD

BRITISH MADE

Correspondence | Address

A Photo of "FELIX," The Super-charged Bradley-Scott Special. Six Speeds, Double Drive to Sidecar wheel, Special Frame, Auto Oiling & Sight feed to all chains, etc. Unbeatable on Rough going, Steep Hills & as a Breakdown Towing Outfit. Designed & Built by Wm Bradley. Addingham Yorks. 1930

*A postcard showing Felix? with Bill's description on the reverse*

He modified his standard Scott Squirrel by making a stronger frame and the addition of a three speed Sturmey-Archer gearbox coupled to the standard two speed unit, making six gears in all–much more suitable for the rough stuff. Then, following the success that he had achieved on the first Felix, Bill turned his attention to two wheel drive but this time driving the sidecar wheel rather than the front. This was achieved by means of a cross-shaft under the sidecar driving that wheel via a short chain. However, the sidecar-wheel-drive system was not instantly successful because, as his colleague Johnny Parkes reported: *'He set off to try it out but at the first corner he came to he went straight into a wall because he had forgotten that he had not fitted a differential gear!'* (In fact, fitting a differential would have been a challenge, even for Bill, but he soon had his tools out to solve the problem by adding a sidecar-passenger-operated clutch!).

He had other spills of course, the worst at Dob Park, Norwood, when his brakes failed and he was pitched over a 10ft banking, crushing his ribs. In a road accident on Leeds Rd, Ilkley, he broke his leg and lost some of the bone but he was soon back riding! On another occasion, during a trial at 'Crankcase Crag', the Scott's two-stroke engine reversed itself during a gear-change and sent the machine hurtling back down the hill at speed. It left the track at the bottom, somersaulted and landed back on its wheels, minus the crew. Bill and his passenger retired badly shaken but received an award for the best sidecar performance!

On this 1926 'Bradley-Scott', he was the first sidecar outfit to climb Hepolite Scar, in May 1926, and the 1in1.62 Post Hill near Pudsey, on Whit Monday 1927, even though he had been up all night repairing the engine which had seized the day before at a Rosedale event. He also climbed a 1in 6 hill at Clifton near Otley with five passengers on board, the notorious, unsurfaced, Park Rash near Kettlewell with four passengers, and Moorend at Kettlewell. Locally, in May 1926, he was the first to climb Beamsley Beacon near Addingham on a motorcycle, with one of his staff, Bert Ward, in the sidecar *(see overleaf)* though they had to stop every now and again to allow the foot-slogging photographers to catch up! He competed in many trials which took place locally, particularly on Addingham Moorside.

*Bill and passenger negotiate a section known as "The Styx" on Addingham Moorside during the 1926 Scott Trial.*

*Bill and Bert Ward about to tackle the ascent of Beamsley Beacon. This 1200ft hill overlooking Addingham gave its name to Bill's 'Beacon Works'.*

# Addingham's Most Inventive Engineer

*Felix conquers Hepolite Scar, the first motorbike & sidecar outfit to do so. The marshal is holding a wedge to put under the wheel when, as he expects, they come to a stop. Needless to say, it was not needed by Felix?*

## The Banking Sidecar and other inventions

Despite having considerable competition success with the two wheel drive 'Felix?', Bill then had the bright idea of devising a linkage to alter the angle of the sidecar wheel on corners, as shown overleaf. The aim was to alter the position of the centre of gravity and avoid the need for the passenger to lean over on corners, and also to elevate or lower the wheel when riding alongside a bank or ditch. To achieve this he had to dispense with the two wheel drive mechanism but this was later re-instated, and the banking mechanism removed, when he had proved that it worked but found that the two-wheel drive was more generally useful for sporting events, as a tow vehicle, and as a gymkhana attraction where Felix? was in great demand, particularly in tugs-of-war. These were brutal pastimes, but fun for the spectators, where competitors' cars were tied to Felix? by tow-rope and tried to pull the little machine backwards. Invariably Bill & Felix? won and the owners of the competing Morris Cowleys, Beans, and other cars of the period, were left with the smoking and non-gripping clutches of their vanquished vehicles!

*With Bert Ward in the banking sidecar at Morton Banks, Airedale*

To make amends for this, many car owners had cause to gratefully remember Felix? as the non-stop machine which rescued them from the depths of some Dales ditch and got them back to civilization and repair at The Beacon Works.

Other unique modifications invented by Bill for this machine included many alternative types of lubrication system, variable port timing, power brakes, a plate-type automatic inlet valve, a pressurised magneto to keep water out of the sparks, and even water heated handlebars for cold weather! *(details in Appendix II)*.

*Post Hill event, 1931    (photo. © C H Wood)*

## Competition medals won by William Bradley

1920 - English Trophy Gold Medal, awarded by the Ilkley Motor Cycle & Light Car Club (IMC&LCC.)

1921 - Autumn Medal Bronze Medal awarded by IMC&LCC

1921 - Dixon Trophy Bronze Medal awarded by IMC&LCC

1923 - Scott Trophy Bronze Medal awarded by I&DMC

1923 - English Trophy Bronze Medal awarded by I&DMC

1924 - Southern Scott Trial Bronze Medal awarded by Camberley & District Motor Club

1924? - Silver Medal awarded by Otley Motor Cycle & Car Club

1925 - Brooks Trophy Bronze Medal awarded by I&DMC

1926 - Dixon Trophy Bronze Medal awarded by I&DMC

1926 - Hepolite Scar Silver Spoon awarded by Bradford & District Motor Club

1928 - Mangham & Moore Bronze Medal awarded by I&DMC

William 'Bill' Bradley

# CHAPTER 4

# WB THE FAMILY MAN
*By Ian Crawshaw, his grandson*

My grandfather William Bradley married Edith Tunnicliffe of Addingham in 1910. Her father John had a grocer's shop on the corner of Church Street and North Street, a building which had once been the Kings Arms public house (then No.14 but now 25 Church St). John Tunnicliffe's wife was Annie, née Roberts, and her aunt Ann Roberts had married John Armstrong of Kettlewell. They had the shop before John Tunnicliffe.

Ann Robert's father, Thomas Roberts, was living with his wife Bethsheba in Low Mill cottages, Addingham, in the 1851 census. They had originated from Barnoldwick and he was listed as an agricultural labourer. Their graves are in the nearby St Peter's Churchyard, as are the Armstrongs'. Edith's Aunt, Maria Dodgson (née Roberts), was still living in North St in the 1940's.

The Bradley family lived with the Tunnicliffes at the shop until John Tunnicliffe died in about 1923 and they then moved to next door-but-one (No.18, now 29), by which time they had three children: my mother Rosa was born in 1911, Jean in 1917 and Jack in 1920. *(Continued p.30, after photographs from the family albums):-*

*The shop on Church St with WB's workshop across the road on the left*

*William & Edith Bradley with their eldest daughter Rosa, born 1911*

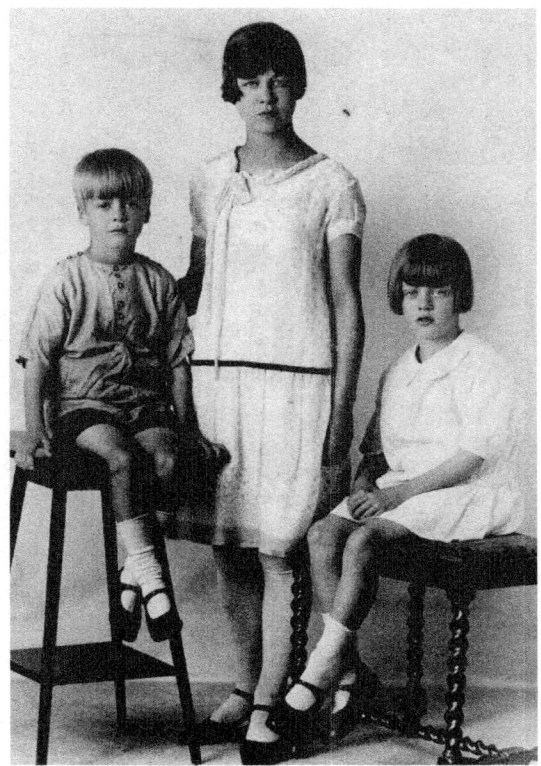

*Jack, Rosa and Jean, 1926*

*The front of 'Lynbrook' in the 1930's. WB was a big lover of animals, here he is (right) with the family pets in the garden*

*Rosa & friends*

*Jean & friends (left), and Jean & Jack (right), in the church field*

## Outings with the children

*WB with Rosa & Jean at Bolton Priory*

# William 'Bill' Bradley

*William with Jack & Jean at the Harrogate Rally 1935*

## Addingham's Most Inventive Engineer

*Rosa on bike with heated handlebars*

*Jean marries Gerald Clapham at St Peters Church, Addingham, 1942*

*With son-in-law Mac Crawshaw and grandchildren Ian & Diana, about 1948*

*Jack marries Peggie Innes, 1948*

*Nana Bradley died in 1952 but Grandpa married Sylvia Parkinson (above) of Adelaide Terrace, Addingham, in 1953*

## Addingham's Most Inventive Engineer

*With Jean & grandchildren Geraldine & Rosalind Clapham*

*Linda Bradley, daughter of Jack & Peggie*

*Dob Park watersplash with Grandson Ian. 1956 Veterans Reunion Trial*

## William 'Bill' Bradley

In the 1930's William and family moved round the corner to 'Lynbrook' on North St, which is opposite the Low School and has Town Beck running through the back garden with two bridges over it. This house and the Church Street cottages are adjacent to the church field and my mother said that they always loved playing in the field, catching fish in the beck and picking the celandines, buttercups and daisies. The fish caught in jam jars on a string were always set free at the end of the day. In later years we, the grandchildren, enjoyed playing there as well; my grandmother (Nana) taught me to ride a very small two wheeler bike along the church path when I was only 3 years old-Grandpa had made the bike, of course! My friend there was Brian Cowan who lived next door to 'Lynbrook'.

My Nana, mid-morning and mid-afternoon, would make tea for the men across at the workshop, always known as "the shop". Usually there were about six employees, two in particular that I can remember were Ivor Town and Pat McShee. My Auntie Jean worked in the office.

Grandpa & Nana Bradley were an important part of our early life and they came down from Addingham to see us at Ilkley every Saturday evening. Sometimes Grandpa would tell my sister and I stories about his adventures with his friends on the moors above Ilkley when he was a boy and also about the years he spent in Canada as a young man or of his motor cycling exploits, now almost 100 years ago in the 1920s.

Our father was away in North Africa during the war so Grandpa was very much a substitute father and he was able to repair any of our broken toys; in fact my Mother swore that I broke them on purpose to give him something to do! Being wartime, there was very little to be had in the way of toys in the shops, but he was always able to make us something for Christmas; I remember that he once made me a crane. We were lucky to have him with us until he was 98 and also thankful that he kept so many photographs and articles about his family, competitive motor cycling and motor cycle modifications, that we could remember him by. Many of these are used in this book.

*Ian Crawshaw*

# CHAPTER 5

# TEXTILE INDUSTRY INVENTIONS

In the 1930s, Bill's inventive skills came to the attention of people in the local textile industry, including nearby Silsden manufacturers who asked him for his help in solving textile making problems. Addingham was then a busy mill village and there were also many other mills in the area, other parts of the West Riding of Yorkshire and elsewhere.
The garage progressively became more an engineering production works called 'William Bradley & Co., Engineer, Beacon Works' and this actually proved more financially rewarding than his previous work.

*The Beacon Works, or 'The Shop', as Bill called it, in 1927*

## *Medal Winning Machine*

Bill Bradley became a bit of a local celebrity when, in 1937, he was awarded a Gold Medal for his inventive skill in solving one of the problems which beset the textile weaving industry.

John Parks, of Main Street, Addingham, was a young engineering apprentice working for Mr Bradley at the time and he described the problem with which Bill was asked to help:-

*'When the mills closed down each weekend from Saturday lunchtime to Monday morning, warp fibres were left stretched across the looms. When the machines were started up again, the extra pull needed to overcome inertia altered the tension and left a blemish on the finished cloth. Mr Bradley's machine was designed to ensure that the warp was maintained automatically at a constant tension when the looms were stopped and started again two days later, from the beginning to the end of the beam.*

*I made a number of components to Mr Bradley's instructions and helped put them together, and I remember travelling with Mr Bradley to mills over the border in Lancashire to install his equipment'.*

The mechanism was fitted to the warp beam of the loom and given the name 'The Bradley Kinetic Brake'. It was claimed to *'work in perfect harmony, and any tendency for variation in the warp tension, which can cause an imperfection in the fabric, is immediately corrected'*. Particularly applicable to the weaving of artificial silk, it was expected to bring down the price of the fabric by eliminating defects. This device was fitted to hundreds of looms in Yorkshire and Lancashire mills.

## *Two Medals*

Bill entered his Kinetic Brake invention in the London exhibition of the Institute of Patentees and was awarded the **Silver Medal**, but when he heard about the **Yorkshire Gold Medal**, (given under the terms of the will of Mr William Hoffman-Wood of Addingham,*(see box)* for the best non-war invention within 30 miles of Leeds, he was determined to win that too, and win it he did, in 1937. The Yorkshire Medal was presented to Bill by the Lord Mayor at a ceremony in the Leeds Town Hall, after which he demonstrated a model of the machine *(opposite)*.

Addingham's Most Inventive Engineer

*Bill (left) demonstrates his invention to Ald.E.J.Clarke (Hoffman-Wood trustee), Capt. G Drury-Coleman (Inst. of Patentees) & the Lord Mayor*

> **Mr William Hoffman-Wood**
> Mr Hoffman-Wood, who was known to Bill (who called him 'Hoffy'), was a Leeds Architect who lived at Hallcroft Hall, Old Ilkley Rd, Addingham, and left generous bequests in his will. As well as the annual 'Yorkshire Gold Medal' that Bill won, he also left money for a 'Leeds Gold Medal' for the best painting, sculpture or architectural work by someone with a parent born within 60 miles of Leeds, and an 'Addingham Gold Medal' for the most valuable discovery in relieving pain or suffering in humanity. On a smaller scale, he left money to give every school child in the area a bank book with one shilling credit, and he also gave what is now the 'Hoffman-Wood Sports Field', between Ilkley Rd and Church St, to Addingham village.

## *Professor Goodman*

Bill was very fortunate to have as a friend Professor John Goodman M.I.C.E. who held the chair at Yorkshire College, Leeds and lived at Lenner House in Beamsley. Prof. Goodman was an eminent civil engineer who was President of the Yorkshire Region of the Institute of Civil Engineers in 1900-1, having won their Miller Prize in 1886.

During the early 1930s he gave Bill financial help and advice on business matters, acting rather like a benevolent uncle. In January 1933 he loaned Bill £100 to help him get his Kinetic Brake textile machines established and in the accompanying letter to Bill he wrote: *'I have every faith in you as an honourable man but, as I have often remarked, if your commercial ability were only equal to your engineering ability you would soon be a millionaire!'*

Bill later allowed the professor to use space at the Beacon Works for his researches.

## *Second World war and after*

During the 1939-45 conflict, the Bradley engineers were involved in aircraft work, making parts for the S.U. Carburetter factory in Low Mill, Addingham, from 1941. This was a 'shadow' factory set up, as a precaution, to duplicate the main S.U. works, then at Shirley, Birmingham, in case of attack. That factory had recently had to move from Adderley due to bomb damage and as S.U. were sole suppliers of carburetters for the Rolls Royce Merlin engines fitted in Spitfire and other war planes security of supply was vital.

Getting back to textile machines after the war, Bill devised the "PRIMM C.R. Cloth Rolling and inspecting machine" *(opposite)*. This machine moved the fabric up over the table under constant tension, and at variable speed, so that defects could be spotted and the roll accurately measured.

The following note from the late Peter Spratt of Addingham describes his experiences with this machine:-

*'When I came to Bradford in 1950 to work in a weaving mill the fabrics (chiefly brocades and damasks for curtains, but also some synthetic fabrics for ladies underwear) were inspected and rolled on a machine designed and manufactured in Addingham by William Bradley. As our business expanded we bought about 3 more machines, but each one included some new innovation! For example, the direct drive to the rolling tube resulted in the cloth moving faster as the diameter of the roll increased, so he fitted a 3-speed Sturmey-Archer bicycle gear to the drive to enable the operator to slow the cloth speed at intervals. For our last machine he geared the drive to a constant speed roller with a sandpaper or rubber surface, the tube of fabric driven by friction on top of this. We also took delivery from Bradley of an automatic warp let-off motion to replace the traditional friction device. Unfortunately this was not very successful, and he was competing with a Swiss textile machinery manufacturer with much greater resources. During this period I met Bradley when he visited the mill. He just loved the challenge of solving mechanical problems.* Peter Spratt, Nov. 2009

# CLOTH ROLLING, INSPECTING and MEASURING MACHINE

Type C.R.
Constant Speed, Reversible

The "PRIMM" C.R. model is of completely new design and modern in appearance. It is light and serviceable, being of all steel construction, and finished in black and green with polished or chromium plated bars and tubes. The driving and transmission gears are housed at one end of the machine in a totally enclosed steel cabinet. All the main shafts and driving members are mounted on ball bearings. It incorporates many new features, some of which are enumerated below.

Particularly suitable for Rayon, Nylon and fine quality piece goods up to 60 inch width, which can be rolled to and from pegs and tubes of 2 inch diameter or boards.

Double acting treadles are situated at the front and rear of machine and winding can be controlled or reversed by the operation of either of these and the reversing lever.

The 3, or 4 speed gear permits constant speeds of 60 to 115 feet per minute, although higher or lower settings can be arranged. The winding tension is maintained automatically, but a No-tension condition obtains while the material passes the measuring device, which is a very desirable feature. Provision is made for "trimming" the machine and to compensate for tight selvedges. Special facilities are provided for the easy threading of the material and engagement with chucks.

The inspection table angle is easily set and secured in position, being well balanced. A measuring unit of our own or other approved make can be supplied, fitted.

Each machine is complete with ¾ h.p. electric motor and control switch, and should give trouble-free operation over long periods and its very high operational efficiency and ease of control are outstanding features.

# WILLIAM BRADLEY & CO.
(Proprietor: William Bradley)

BEACON WORKS, ADDINGHAM, ILKLEY, YORKS.

Telephone: Addingham 258.

*Advertisement for the Bradley inspecting and rolling machine*

William 'Bill' Bradley

# Chapter 6

## The end of the long, long, road

Bill Bradley finally closed his 'shop' commercially in the late 1950s (he was over 70 by then), probably because of the decline of the textile industry, but he still kept thinking up new projects and would go down and 'tinker around', with a tin of soup for lunch, until his sight failed in his 80s. He remained physically fit, however, and when 92 he walked two miles to a meeting, and refused a lift home afterwards!

So we come to the end of the remarkable career of the plumber's son from Ilkley who developed into an amazingly clever and inventive engineer who delighted in the challenge of solving technical problems that would defeat most skilled and qualified technicians. What is more, Bill could turn these ideas into working machines, often against the clock.
His love of motorcycles never left him, as shown by the final photographs which follow, and his earlier achievements in motorcycle competitions were outstanding. *William 'Bill' Bradley was, indeed, Addingham's Most Inventive Engineer.*

He sold the premises in 1971 and the buildings were used for a time as a farm clothing shop but were demolished in 1986 and the area re-developed for housing (including Sawyer's Garth).
**We end with some final pictures from the Bradley family albums:-**

*Bill with Great-Grandchildren Jacqueline & Richard Crawshaw at Masham Steam Rally 1972 (above & below)*

## Family group for WB's 90th. Birthday

Back row: Ian Crawshaw, Gerald Clapham, Jack Bradley, Peggie Bradley (née Innes), Rosalind Wilson (née Clapham), Leonard Bradley (nephew), Ada Barnes (cousin), George Bradley (brother).

Seated: Christina Crawshaw (née Kendall), Jean Clapham (née Bradley), William Bradley, Rosa Crawshaw (née Bradley), Ethel Barnes (cousin).

Kneeling: great-grandchildren: Jacqueline Crawshaw, Victoria Crawshaw, Richard Crawshaw.

# William 'Bill' Bradley

*Bill outside the building when a clothing shop*

*Demolition in 1986, former school on the right*

Addingham's Most Inventive Engineer

# _William 'Bill' Bradley died in May 1983 at the age of 98_

William 'Bill' Bradley

# Appendix I

## 'Felix'

*(Re-produced from Motor Cycle Sport magazine, November 1965)*

Felix was a Raleigh; one of those excellent little black and gold outside-flywheel side-valves of the type ridden to such good effect by Marjorie Cottle and Hugh Gibson, amongst others. Bill Bradley decided that doubling-up the drive to the earth's surface, whatever the latter might consist of, would at least double the chances of a Felix-style passage. But to drive a steering front wheel from the existing transmission line of convention is no mean feat in itself; to design all the components, and manufacture the lot in under two weeks, seems a near-miracle but, as far as Bill Bradley was concerned, it was just another interesting exercise in precision engineering. A 1in wide sprocket, riveted to the existing rear-drive sprocket, was the start of the front wheel drive. From this a chain was run over a pair of adjustable jockeys to the input end of a Hooke's-type universal joint, the drive member of which ran in a frame bracket. From the output member of the joint, carried in a front-fork bracket, another sprocket and chain took the drive down to the front wheel. To prevent excessive whip of the first stage, 6ft·long, chain, and of course for protection, its two long runs under the tank, were taken through fibre tubes.

The drawing (overleaf), reproduced from Mr Bradley's original, shows the details clearly. The two jockeys below the saddle are adapted from bicycle freewheels and run on ball-bearings. They are mounted in two plates which are pivoted on a frame-bracket so as to allow adjustment by a turnbuckle device.

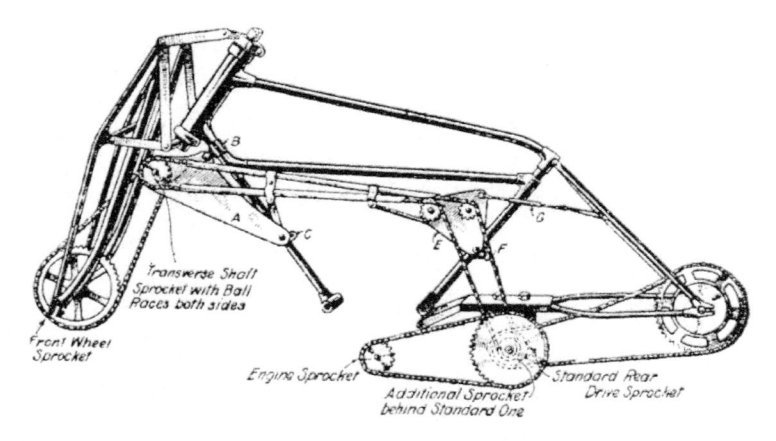

[Diagram of frame with labels: Transverse Shaft Sprocket with Ball Races both sides; Front Wheel Sprocket; Engine Sprocket; Additional Sprocket behind Standard One; Standard Rear Drive Sprocket]

The steering head universal joint (below) is composed of two chain sprockets, three self-aligning ball bearings, and the Hooke's-type universal joint in the centre. The input shaft has two support plates for its bearings, carried on the front down-tube of the frame. The central axis of the joint is of course on the steering-head centre-line, the maximum angularity being 27 degrees to either side.

Though this is certainly a somewhat limited lock, it still represents a turning radius of 10ft and Bill evidently had his own way of coping with anything more acute than this. The output

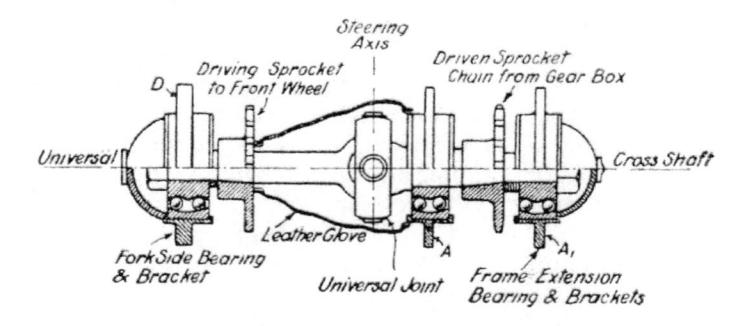

[Diagram of steering head universal joint with labels: Steering Axis; Driving Sprocket to Front Wheel; Driven Sprocket Chain from Gear Box; Universal; Cross Shaft; Fork Side Bearing & Bracket; Leather Glove; Universal Joint; Frame Extension Bearing & Brackets]

*Reproduction of the original Bradley sketch and drawing*
A    *Frame bracket, steering point input shaft*
BC  *Attachment points for A*
D    *Fork bracket, steering joint output shaft*
E    *Frame bracket, jockey sprockets*
F    *Attachment point for E*
G    *Adjustment turnbuckle for jockeys*

shaft of the joint is carried on the third ball bearing, housed in a bracket which forms part of the offside lower-fork shackle.

The second chain, 3ft in length, takes the drive to a front wheel sprocket. The forks are rigid, but in discussing this point Bill made it very evident that spring forks could have been adapted without difficulty by a suitable modification to the output end of the drive. In fact he found no adverse effect from the lack of springing, in the usual conditions common to Felix's enterprises.

# Appendix II

# The 1925 Bradley-Scott: 'Felix?'

## A Mobile Test Bed

*In Appendix I was the story of 'Felix', the solo machine, but Bill was always thinking up new ideas which were put into practice on Felix? - a sidecar outfit but again built to challenge the best in trials competitions*

*This time he based his machine on a Scott Squirrel motorcycle and sidecar outfit made locally at Saltaire, Bradford. Scott bikes were made for many years and were of a unique design, being two stroke engines with water cooling – very advanced for the time.*

*The following report, from Motorcycle Sport Magazine, September 1966, explains the ingenious modifications and novel design features that he fitted to the machine:*

The frame, completely duplicated, was not unlike the Scott pattern which appeared several months later. It would seem, in fairness, that one or two Great Minds at Saltaire were also thinking on Bradley lines, though not quite to the same extremes. At the base, a stout steel tray carries the crankcase bottom at its fore end and duplex chain stays at the rear. A Scott two-chain countershaft is mounted in a pair of near-vertical steel straps running between the engine top bolt and the tray. Behind the countershaft is located a standard Sturmey-Archer three-speed gearbox; thus six ratios, for a start! The saddle is carried on a pyramid of duplex seat tubes and back stays, and from the apex a further pair of tubes runs forward to the top and bottom of the steering head. The radiator is seated on a rubber-padded anti-vibration mounting.

## Six Speeds

Apart from the frame, the transmission is obviously one of the most interesting features. The normal Scott two-speed gear has its two primary chains to the engine arranged as usual, but at shorter centres. From the countershaft nearside a short chain takes the power to the standard Sturmey-Archer clutch, and thence from the box output, by chain to a rear sprocket with a double row of teeth. From this rear sprocket a short chain drives forwards to a transverse counter-shaft carried in a large-diameter tube across to the sidecar wheel, which latter is driven by another short chain from the other end of the shaft. By this arrangement the sidecar wheel can be positioned forward relatively to the rear wheel, to any desired extent. A hand-operated dog-clutch is housed inside the tube, and the latter also acts as a "torque tube," adding strength and rigidity to the Bradley-designed sidecar chassis.

In the Sturmey box, as bought, the ratios were 1:1, 1:8 and 3:6, which, given a 4.5:1 top gear, would provide overall ratios of 4.5, 8.1 and 16.2. By using a specially cut 34 tooth low-speed sprocket on the two-speed countershaft, Bill was able to obtain another set of ratios to come nicely in between these three, giving six steps capable of coping with any requirements of load, gradient, and acceleration. The final set is 4.5, 6.1, 8.1, 11.0, 16.2 and 22.

Felix, as has been remarked, developed fast. Pedal operation of the two-speed gear gave place to handlebar control by flexible cable, with the gear converted to simple dog engagement; the built-in friction clutches being deemed superfluous anyway. Pneumatic hubs, invented and patented by C Handel, a fellow Yorkshireman from Skipton, were fitted. As the sketch shows, these hubs incorporated a D-section rubber tube, inflated by a tyre pump via a valve protruding from the hub shell. In addition to equipping

Felix, Bill made several sets at his works for trial by car manufacturers.

The sidecar-wheel-drive also received some redesigning attention. The short centre chain drives from each end of the transverse shaft were scrapped, the dog clutch discarded, and the whole converted to wedge-gearing drive. Each of the end drives now comprised a large diameter mild-steel wedge-wheel having its circumference of vee-section, engaging a vee-groove pinion. The pinions were mounted on the transverse shaft, and the latter was arranged to lie ahead of the rear wheel wedge-drive and behind the sidecar-wheel ditto. Thus, by rocking the shaft horizontally about its mid-point by a small amount, both wedge-drives could be disengaged. Simple, as positive as you could want, and with nothing to go wrong.

*WB with Ralph Townson, Moorend, Kettlewell, 1927*

However, when Mr. Bradley decided to experiment with 'banking' effects, the sidecar-wheel-drive was temporarily suspended. Bill wanted to investigate the effects of banking rather as a mathematical exercise, as he felt that certain people were playing about with these rather frightening devices without appreciating all the snags, not that such a revelation was likely to put them off! His idea for such a design stipulated retention of the centre of gravity within the track of the outfit, complete control by the driver only, and banking by engine power in either direction of lean.

The mechanism of the Auto-Flexi, as the chassis is called, is carried on a tube parallel with the nearside of the machine. At each end of the tube a crank rotates in bearings, the two cranks being synchronized by a pulley-and-wire-rope drive. The front end of the sidecar chassis is attached in a bearing to the throw of the front crank, while at the rear a transverse shaft is coupled to the throw. At its other end this shaft carries the sidecar wheel on a third throw, as shown in the sketch. Synchronized rotation of the two coupled cranks will tilt the chassis, to a maximum of 18 degrees either way. Tests showed that 14 degrees was quite sufficient, and under these

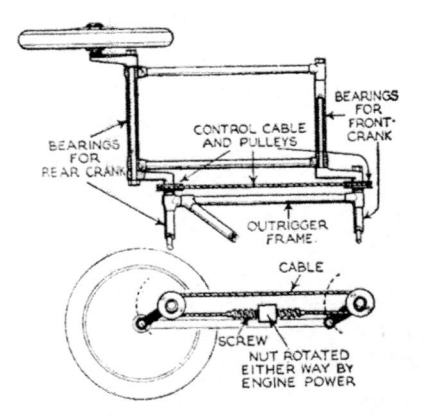

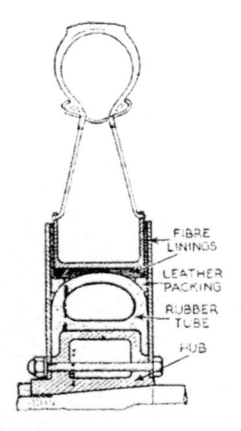

*'Auto-Flexi' banking sidecar mechanism*     *Handel pneumatic hub*

conditions some interesting figures emerged relating to the static load carried by the road wheels.

With the machine upright and fully laden, the weight carried respectively by the machine and sidecar wheels is 348 lb and 175 lb, totalling 523 lb. On banking 14 degrees to the left, these figures become 270 lb and 273 lb, and on banking the same angle to the right, 460 lb and 60 lb. The significance is that, in either direction of bank, about 100lb weight is transferred from one wheel to the other, and the effect of this, particularly on a left hand turn, will be appreciated by all chair-men.

Within the track of about 40in the centre of gravity moves transversely for a total distance of 9in, as the outfit is banked from left to right, or vice versa, and no acrobatics whatsoever were required on the part of the passenger to assist cornering.

**Power drive**
The steel cable which synchronizes the two cranks serves also to turn them. The pulley adjacent to each crank is grooved to allow a wrap-round of a turn-and-a-half, no slip being ever experienced. On its top run the cable is provided with a turnbuckle tensioner. At the lower run the cable ends are firmly attached to each end of a quick-threaded bar enclosed in a tube and carrying a large nut at its centre. This nut is restrained against lateral movement and is rotated by a worm engaging teeth cut in its periphery. The worm is driven by means of a simple reversible friction drive, whose input shaft is coupled to the Sturmey clutch centre by a flexible coupling. The reversing drive is controlled by foot pressure on the forward end of each footboard, left for left and right for right bank.

When foot pressure is released the outfit remains at the angle assumed, since the nut-and-thread cable drive is irreversible. The banking mechanism absorbed very little power, no 'braking' effect being observable, while action was extremely rapid in changing from one angle to the other.

There are several other intriguing characteristics of the design. On high cambered roads the machine could be trimmed to a fixed angle so as to cancel steering drag, while on rough and narrow tracks the sidecar wheel was lifted to run along a high verge, with the motorcycle at a lower level but still upright.

The next step would have been to combine the banking system with sidecar wheel drive; not an easy problem to solve but well within the Bradley resources. However, at this stage, more urgent jobs awaited the Beacon Works, and in view of its more general usefulness in sporting events two-wheel traction was restored and the banking gear discarded. Power braking was installed, by converting the rear-brake anchor plate to operate as a servo-motor. The plate is free to rotate through a limited angle under the torque applied to it when the pedal is depressed. In rotating, the plate actuates flexible cables which apply the front and sidecar brakes. In addition, a hand-brake lever is provided, both for parking and for use instead of the pedal. The whole system is fully adjustable and extra leverage is available on the front brake, if necessary, from a normal separate handlebar control.

While Mr. Bradley thought a lot of both Scott's original engine design and its subsequent development he did not by any means consider it incapable of improvement. Over a lengthy period he experimented, for example, with many types of lubrication system: petroil with circulating pipes, duplex mechanical oil pump, and visible suction drip feed with hand-setting. (As most trials riders on Scotts found at that period, the last named was most generally satisfactory.) He also fitted the engine with movable cylinder liners, which could be adjusted from outside to provide variable port timing. A further try-out comprised an exhaust-pipe throttle valve interconnected with the carburettor, to investigate the effect of varying exhaust back-pressure at small throttle openings.

For winter comfort Bill designed a pair of water-heated handlebars, with a separate water-circuit via a heat exchanger coiled inside the cylinder head jacket, and a circulating pump of diaphragm type operated by crankcase depression, all manufactured on the spot.

But probably the most interesting engine modification, and one which should surely be probed further, was his plate type automatic inlet valve, designed for mounting on each crankcase cover-plate. The advantages conferred by this were immediately apparent, as one photograph shows. Even Saltaire was *mildly* interested! Several decades later the same applies-Scott enthusiasts who have knowledge of the device have barely been able to summon a yawn.'

# Appendix III

# Scott Motorcycles

The Scott Motorcycle Company was owned by Scott Motors (Saltaire) Limited, Shipley, West Yorkshire, and was a well-known producer of motorcycles and light engines for industry. Founded by Alfred Angas Scott in 1908 as the Scott Engineering Company, Scott motorcycles were produced until 1978.

Scott designed and patented a vertical twin two-stroke engine in 1904, and patented the familiar Scott motorcycle frame in 1908 designed to use that engine and achieve a low centre of gravity. The resulting motorcycle was launched in 1908 featuring a 450cc two-stroke twin-cylinder water-cooled engine. Innovative features included a patented two-speed chain transmission in which the alternative ratios were selected by clutches operated by a rocking foot pedal and a kick start also patented. The first few machines to his design were produced by Bradford based car firm Jowett in 1908 but soon after he set up as a manufacturer in his own right at the Mornington Works, Grosvenor Road, Bradford.

While Scott's production machines were marketed as a kind of luxury "wheeled horse" for the Edwardian Gentleman, there was valuable publicity to be had in competition success and the early Scott motorcycles were so powerful that they often easily beat four-stroke motorcycles of the same capacity. After Scott's victory at the 1908 Wass Bank hillclimb, the Auto-Cycle Union handicapped their motorcycles by multiplying their cubic capacity by 1.32 for competitive purposes, which resulted in good, free advertising for Scott. The handicap was lifted three years later.

Scott made several appearances at the Isle of Man TT Races between 1910 and 1914 with specially built racing machines. In 1910 a Scott was the first two-stroke motorcycle ever to complete a full TT course under race conditions and in 1911 a Scott ridden by Frank Phillip gained the TT lap record of 50.11 mph continuous average speed. This winning streak continued with Scott's being the fastest machines in 1912, 1913, and 1914 and winning the event in 1912 and 1913. From 1911 to 1914 Scott's Tourist Trophy racers used rotary valves to control the inlet and transfer phases of the two-stroke cycle. In 1911 the engine was controlled by advancing or retarding the valve timing and not by the throttle. Scott reverted to throttle control in 1912, giving the rotary valves a fixed gear drive in the same year.

Scott produced some gun carriages during the Great War and after the war production restarted with the 532 cc Standard Tourer and in 1922 Scott introduced the Squirrel, its first sporting model to be offered to the general public. This had a slightly smaller 486 cc engine to bring it within the 500 cc competition limit but, with aluminium pistons and careful preparation, it produced more power. In addition, many heavy accessories such as foot boards and leg shields which had been fitted to the touring models were dispensed with, making it a very light and competitive motorcycle. It was followed by the Super Squirrel, with a further revised engine of 498 cc or 596 cc, which was the mainstay of production in the mid-1920s. Although they never regained their pre-war form, Scotts continued to compete successfully in sporting events scoring a 3-4 in the 1922 TT and a third in 1924. A three-speed gearbox with conventional clutch was offered from 1923 and in this form the machine had some success as a trials motorcycle, notably the modified machine made and used by Bill Bradley.

*(Reproduced from Wikipedia.com under Creative Commons licence)*

*1923 486cc Scott Squirrel*
*Yesterday's Antique Motorcycles en Classic Motorcycle Archive*

# ABOUT THE AUTHORS

*Don Barrett*

Having been born and brought up in Cambridge, Don started work at Vauxhall Motors in Luton, becoming a metallurgist there, and initially used to travel home at weekends on motorcycles (first a BSA Bantam and then a Triumph Tiger Cub). He later graduated to cars, particularly an early BMC Minivan which was modified and used for sprints, hillclimbs and autocross events. With this background he found the production of this book a very interesting exercise!

In 1995 he and his wife Lesley moved up to Addingham, their three boys having flown the nest, and he has since taken a keen interest in local, and particularly industrial, history and the Addingham Civic Society. He maintains the archive of village photographs and the village website–*addingham.info*.


*Ian Crawshaw*

Ian was born in 1939 and has lived in Ilkley since 1940. After leaving school he went to work as a draughtsman at Spooner's, an engineering firm in Ilkley, retiring after being with them for 47 years.

As well as geology, and railways he is interested in local and family history and has been able to draw on the latter to tell the story of his Grandfather's life.

He is married to Christina, an Ilkley girl, and they have three children and seven grown up grandchildren, who live both locally and in Australia.

William 'Bill' Bradley

Printed in Great Britain
by Amazon